PYTHON PATTERN PROGRAMS

ANJALI SHARMA

Mumma & Abhishesk,

If there's one thing I wish for you to remember, it's that I love you both very much.

OM NAMAH SHIVAYE!!!

Contents

Preface

Python is a very elegant, concise and powerful programming language, which is designed for programmer productivity, code reusablility, readability and software quality.

This book contains five chapters, each dedicated to different types of pattern programs which are meant to test any programmers logical ability and depth of programming knowledge. This book is mainly desgined to allow students to get all important patterns and logics that they require to practice.

There are a couple of things that will be required to progress through this book. First the basic knowledge of python loops structures and second the decision statements. If you that much you are good to go.

I have tried to keep the content short and precice, with just code and the output. The better way to follow will be understanding the pattern, developing the logic and then refering to the code given along side the pattern. I encourage you to type the code!

Now let's get coding!

Acknowledgements

The work presented in this book would not have been possible without my close association with many people. I take this opportunity to extend my sincere gratitude and appreciation to all those who made this book possible.

I owe my deepest gratitude towards my mother Mrs. Vandana Sharma for her selfless support and encouragement. This book is indeed a realization of her dream. Her infallible love and support has always been my strength.

I would like to thank my husband Mr. Abhishek Bhardwaj for tolerating me throughout the whole process of writing this book. A huge thanks to you, I appreciate every thing you have done for me.

Finally, my greatest regards to the Almighty for bestowing upon me the courage to face the complexities of life and complete my dissertation successfully.

## CHAPTER ONE

STAR PATTERNS

Q1. Write a python program to draw the Solid Rectangle pattern
Solution:

```python
r=int(input("Enter the number of rows:"))
c=int(input("Enter the number of colunms:"))
for i in range(r):
for j in range(c):
print("*",end="")
print()
```

```
Enter the number of rows:4
Enter the number of colunms:16

****************
****************
****************
****************
```

Output of Q1

Q2. Write a python program to draw the Hollow Rectangle pattern
Solution:

```python
r=int(input("Enter the number of rows:"))
c=int(input("Enter the number of colunms:"))
for i in range(1,r+1):
for j in range(1,c+1):
if i==1 or i==r or j==1 or j==c:
```

```
print("*",end="")
else:
print(" ",end="")
print()
```

```
Enter the number of rows:4
Enter the number of colunms:16
****************
*              *
*              *
****************
```

Output of Q2

Q3. Write a python program to print rectangle with diagonal pattern
Solution:

```
r=int(input("Enter the number of rows:"))
for i in range(1,r+1):
for j in range(1,r+1):
if i==1 or i==r or j==1 or j==r or i==j or (i+j)==r+1:
print("*",end="")
else:
print(" ",end="")
print()
```

```
Enter the number of rows:6
******
**  **
* ** *
* ** *
**  **
******
```

Output of Q3

Q4. Write a python program to print a rhombus of stars

Solution:
```python
r=int(input("Enter the number of rows:"))
for i in range(1,r+1):
for j in range(1,r-i+1):
print(" ",end="" )
for j in range(1,r+1):
print("*",end="")
print()
```

```
Enter the number of rows:5
    *****
     *****
      *****
       *****
        *****
```

Output of Q4

Q5. Write a python program to print a hollow rhombus of stars
Solution:
```python
r=int(input("Enter the number of rows:"))
for i in range(1,r+1):
for j in range(1,r-i+1):
print(" ",end="")
for j in range(1,r+1):
if i==1 or i==r:
print("*",end="")
else:
if j==1 or j==r:
print("*",end="")
else:
print(" ",end="")
print()
```

```
Enter the number of rows:5
*****
*   *
*   *
*   *
*****
```

Output of Q5

Q6. Write a python program to print a rhombus of stars (Opposite tilt)
Solution:

```python
r=int(input("Enter the number of rows:"))
for i in range(1,r+1):
for j in range(0,i-1):
print(" ",end="")
for j in range(1,r+1):
print("*",end="")
print()
```

```
Enter the number of rows:5
*****
 *****
  *****
   *****
    *****
```

Output of Q6

Q7. Write a python program to draw the Right angle Triangle pattern
Solution:

```python
n=int(input("Enter the number of rows: "))
for i in range(1,n+1):
for j in range(1,i+1):
print("*",end=" ")
print()
```

```
Enter the number of rows: 5
*

* *

* * *

* * * *

* * * * *
```

Output of Q7

Q8. Write a python program to draw the Mirror image of Right angle Triangle pattern

Solution:

```
r=int(input("Enter the number of rows:"))
for i in range(1,r+1):
for j in range(1,r-i+1):
print(" ",end="" )
for j in range(1,i+1):
print("*",end="")
print()
```

```
Enter the number of rows:5
    *
   **
  ***
 ****
*****
```

Output of Q8

Q9. Write a python program to draw the Right angle triangle with odd "*" in each row

Solution:

```
n=int(input("Enter the number of rows"))
m=1
for i in range(1,n+1):
```

```python
for j in range(1,m+1):
print("*",end=" ")
m=m+2
print()
```

```
Enter the number of rows: 5
*

* * *

* * * * *

* * * * * * *

* * * * * * * * *
```

Output of Q9

Q10. Write a python program to draw Inverted right angle triangle
Solution:
```python
n=int(input("Enter the number of rows"))
for i in range(n+1,0,-1):
for j in range(i,0,-1):
print("*",end=" ")
print()
```

```
Enter the number of rows: 5
******
*****
****
***
**
*
```

Output of Q10

Q11. Write a python program to draw mirror image of Inverted right angle triangle
Solution:
```python
n=int(input("Enter the number of rows: "))
for i in range(n+1,0,-1):
```

```python
for j in range(0,(n+1)-i):
print(" ",end="")
for j in range(i,1,-1):
print('*',end="")
print()
```

```
Enter the number of rows: 5
*****
 ****
  ***
   **
    *
```

Output of Q11

Q12. Write a python program to print Hollow right angle triangle
Solution:

```python
n=int(input("Enter the number of rows:"))
for i in range(0,n):
for j in range(0,n):
if j==0 or i==n-1 or i==j:
print("*",end="")
else:
print(" ",end="")
print()
```

```
Enter the number of rows:6
*
**
* *
*  *
*   *
******
```

Output of Q12

Q13. Write a python program to print mirror image of Hollow right angle triangle

Solution:

```
n=int(input("Enter the number of rows:"))
for i in range(1,n+1):
for j in range(1,n+1):
if i==n or j==n or (i+j)==n+1:
print("*",end="")
else:
print(" ",end="")
print()
```

```
Enter the number of rows:6
     *
    **
   * *
  *  *
 *   *
******
```

Output of Q13

Q14. Write a python program to print Inverted right angle triangle

Solution:

```
n=int(input("Enter the number of rows:"))
for i in range(1,n+1):
for j in range(1,n+1):
if i==1 or j==1 or (i+j)==n+1:
print("*",end="")
else:
print(" ",end="")
print()
```

```
Enter the number of rows:6
******
*     *
*    *
*   *
**
*
```

Output of Q14

Q15. Write a python program to draw Mirror image of Hollow inverted right angle triangle
Solution:
```
n=int(input("Enter the number of rows:"))
for i in range(1,n+1):
for j in range(1,n+1):
if i==1 or j==n or i==j:
print("*",end="")
else:
print(" ",end="")
print()
```

```
Enter the number of rows:6
******
   *     *
    *    *
     *  *
      **
       *
```

Output of Q15

Q16. Write a python program to draw the Pyramid Pattern.
Solution:

```
    n=int(input("Enter the number of rows"))
for i in range(0,n):
for j in range(0,n-i-1):
print(end=" ")
for k in range(0,i+1):
print("*",end=" ")
print()
```

```
Enter the number of rows5
    *
   * *
  * * *
 * * * *
* * * * *
```

Output of Q16

Q17. Write a python program to draw the following pattern (Inverted Pyramid)

Solution:

```
n=int(input("Enter the number of rows"))
for i in range(n,0,-1):
for j in range(0,n-i):
print(end=" ")
for k in range(0,i):
print("*",end=" ")
print()
```

```
Enter the number of rows5
* * * * *
 * * * *
  * * *
   * *
    *
```

Output of Q17

Q18. Write a python program to draw the following pattern (hollow pyramid)

Solution:

```python
n=int(input("Enter the number of rows "))
for i in range(1,n+1):
for j in range(1,2*n):
if i==n or (i+j)==n+1 or (j-i)==n-1:
print("*",end="")
else:
print(end=" ")
print()
```

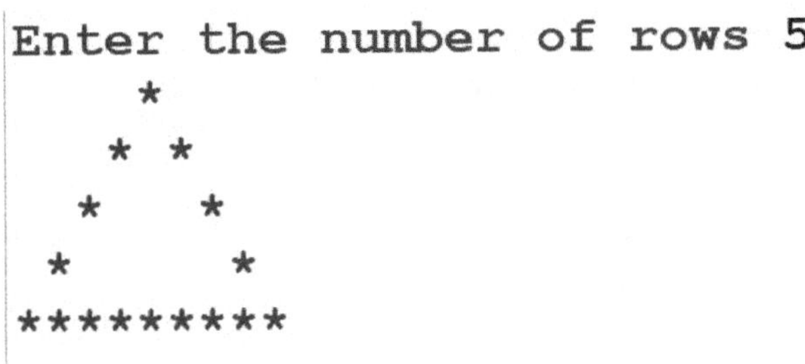

Output of Q18

Q19. Write a python program to print stars '*' in diamond shape.

Solution:

```python
n=int(input("Enter the number of rows"))
for i in range(n):
print(" "*(n-i-1)+"* "*(i+1))
for j in range(n-1,0,-1):
print(" "*(n-j)+"* "*(j))
```

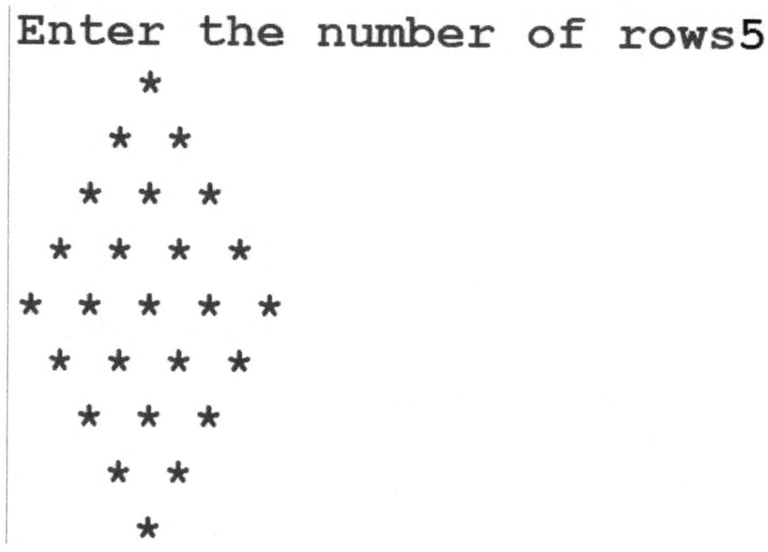

Output of Q19

Q20. Write a python program to print a Hollow diamond of "*"
Solution:

```python
n=int(input("Enter the number of rows "))
for i in range(0,n):
for j in range(0,n):
if (i+j)==(n-1)/2 or (j-i)==(n-1)/2 or (i+j)==n+1 or (i-j)==(n-1)/2:
print("*",end="")
else:
print(end=" ")
print()
```

```
Enter the number of rows 5
    *
   *  *
  *      *
   *  *
    *
```

Output of Q20

Q21. Write a python program to print solid half diamond
Solution:
```
n=int(input("Enter the number of rows"))
for i in range(1,n+1):
for j in range(1,n+1-i):
print(end="")
for j in range(1,i):
print("*", end="")
print()
for i in range(n,0,-1):
for j in range(1,n-1):
print(end="")
for j in range(1,i):
print("*", end="")
print()
```

```
Enter the number of rows6
```

```
*
**
***
****
*****
*****
****
***
**
*
```

Output of Q21

Q22. Write a python program to print the given pattern (Arrow)
Solution:
```python
n=int(input("Enter the number of rows:"))
for i in range(n+n-1):
s=i
if i >=n:
s = n+n-i-2
for j in range(s+s):
if j < s:
print(" ",end="")
else:
print("*",end="")
print()
```

```
Enter the number of rows:6
```

```
    *
   **
  ***
 ****
*****
 ****
  ***
   **
    *
```

Output of Q22

Q23. Write a python program to print glass hour pattern
Solution:
n=int(input("Enter the number of rows:"))
k = n - 2
for i in range(n, -1 , -1):
for j in range(k , 0 , -1):
print(end=" ")
k = k + 1
for j in range(0, i+1):
print("* " , end="")
print()
k = 2 * n - 2
for i in range(0 , n+1):
for j in range(0 , k):
print(end=" ")
k = k - 1
for j in range(0, i + 1):
print("* ", end="")
print()

```
Enter the number of rows:4
  *  *  *  *  *
    *  *  *  *
      *  *  *
        *  *
          *
          *
        *  *
      *  *  *
    *  *  *  *
  *  *  *  *  *
```

Output of Q23

## CHAPTER TWO

NUMBER PATTERNS

Q1. Write a python program to draw the following pattern

```
1 2 3 4 5
1 2 3 4 5
1 2 3 4 5
1 2 3 4 5
1 2 3 4 5
```

Solution:

```python
r=int(input("Enter the number of rows:"))
c=int(input("Enter the number of cols:"))
for i in range(1,r+1):
for j in range(1,c+1):
print(j,end="")
print()
```

Note: For a different pattern replace "j" with "i"

```
Enter the number of rows:5
Enter the number of cols:5
12345
12345
12345
12345
12345
```

Output of Q1

```
Enter the number of rows:5
Enter the number of cols:5
11111
22222
33333
44444
55555
```

when "j" is replaced with "i"

Q2. Write a python program to print the given pattern
11011
11011
00000
11011
11011
Solution:

```
num=int(input("Enter the number of rows:"))
for i in range(num):
for j in range(num):
if i==int((num)/2) or j==int((num)/2):
print(0,end="")
else:
print(1,end="")
print()
```

```
Enter the number of rows:5
11011
11011
00000
11011
11011
```

Output of Q2

Q3. Write a python program to print the given pattern
11111
11111
11011
11111
11111
Solution:
num=int(input("Enter the number of rows:"))
nr=1
nc=1
for i in range(num):
for j in range(num):
if i==int((num)/2)==j:
print(0,end="")
else:
print(1,end="")
print()

```
Enter the number of rows:5
11111
11111
11011
11111
11111
```

Output of Q3

Q4. Write a python program to print the given pattern
11111
10001
10001
10001
11111
Solution:
num=int(input("Enter the number of rows:"))
nr=1
nc=1

```python
for i in range(1,num+1):
for j in range(1,num+1):
if i==1 or j==1 or i==num or j==num:
print(1,end="")
else:
print(0,end="")
print()
```

```
Enter the number of rows:5
11111
10001
10001
10001
11111
```

Output of Q4

Q5. Write a python program to print the given pattern
10001
01010
00100
01010
10001
Solution:

```python
num=int(input("Enter the number of rows:"))
nr=1
nc=1
for i in range(1,num+1):
for j in range(1,num+1):
if i==j or (i+j)==num+1:
print(1,end="")
else:
print(0,end="")
print()
```

```
Enter the number of rows:5
10001
01010
00100
01010
10001
```

Output of Q5

Q6. Write a python program to print the given pattern
12345
23456
34567
45678
56789
Solution:
num=int(input("Enter the number of rows:"))
nr=1
nc=1
for i in range(1,num+1):
for j in range(1,num+1):
print(nr,end="")
nr += 1
nc += 1
nr = nc
print()

```
Enter the number of rows:5
12345
23456
34567
45678
56789
```

Output of Q6

Q7. Write a python program to print the given pattern

55555

54444

54333

54322

54321

Solution:

```python
num=int(input("Enter the number of rows:"))
for i in range(1,num+1):
for j in range(num,num-i,-1):
print(j,end="")
for j in range(1,num-i+1):
print(num-i+1,end="")
print()
```

```
Enter the number of rows:5
55555
54444
54333
54322
54321
```

Output of Q7

Q8. Write a python program to print the given pattern

Solution:

```python
num=int(input("Enter the number of rows:"))
nr=1
nc=1
for i in range(num):
for j in range(num):
if i==int((num)/2):
print(nr,end="")
nr=nr+1
if i==j:
nc=nc+1
```

```
elif j==int((num)/2):
print(nc,end="")
nc=nc+1
else:
print(" ",end="")
print()
```

```
Enter the number of rows:5
    1
    2
12345
    4
    5
```

Output of Q8

Q9. Write a python program to draw the following pattern
Solution:
```
n=int(input("Enter the value of N:"))
for i in range(1,n+1):
for j in range(1,i):
print(" ",end="")
print(i,end="")
for j in range(1,(n-i)*2):
print(" ",end="")
if(i!=n):
print(i,end="")
print()
for i in range(n-1,0,-1):
for j in range(1,i):
print(" ",end="")
print(i,end="")
for j in range(1,(n-i)*2):
print(" ",end="")
print(i,end="")
print()
```

```
Enter the value of N:5
1           1
  2       2
    3   3
      4 4
        5
      4 4
    3   3
  2       2
1           1
```

Output of Q9

Q10. **Write a python program to draw the following pattern**
Solution:
```python
n=int(input("Enter the value of N:"))
nr=1
for i in range(1,n+1):
for j in range(1,i):
print(" ",end="")
print(nr,end="")
for j in range(1,(n-i)*2):
print(" ",end="")
if(i!=n):
print(nr,end="")
nr += 1
print()
for i in range(n-1,0,-1):
for j in range(1,i):
print(" ",end="")
print(nr,end="")
for j in range(1,(n-i)*2):
print(" ",end="")
print(nr,end="")
nr += 1
print()
```

```
Enter the value of N:5
1       .   1
  2           2
    3       3
      4 4
        5
      6 6
    7       7
  8           8
9               9
```

Output of Q10

Q11. Write a python program to print the given pattern
1 2 3 4 5
6 7 8 9 10
11 12 13 14 15
16 17 18 19 20
21 22 23 24 25
r=int(input("Enter the number of rows:"))
c=int(input("Enter the number of cols:"))
curr = 1
for i in range(1,r+1):
for j in range(1,c+1):
print(format(curr,"4d"),end="")
curr += 1
print()

```
Enter the number of rows:5
Enter the number of cols:5
    1    2    3    4    5
    6    7    8    9   10
   11   12   13   14   15
   16   17   18   19   20
   21   22   23   24   25
```

Output of Q11

Q12. Write a python program to print the given pattern

```
1 2 3 4 5
16 17 18 19 6
15 24 25 20 7
14 23 22 21 8
13 12 11 10 9
num=int(input("Enter the number of rows:"))
n_list=[[0 for x in range(num)] for y in range(num)]
n=1
low=0
high=num-1
count=int((num+1)/2)
for i in range(count):
for j in range(low,high+1):
n_list[i][j]=n
n = n+1
for j in range(low+1,high+1):
n_list[j][high]=n
n = n+1
for j in range(high-1,low-1,-1):
n_list[high][j]=n
n = n+1
for j in range(high-1,low,-1):
n_list[j][low]=n
n = n+1
low = low+1
high = high-1
for i in range(num):
for j in range(num):
print(format(n_list[i][j],"4d"),end=" ")
print()
```

```
Enter the number of rows:5
   1     2     3     4     5
  16    17    18    19     6
  15    24    25    20     7
  14    23    22    21     8
  13    12    11    10     9
```

Output of Q12

Q13. Write a python program to print the given pattern
3 3 3 3 3
3 2 2 2 3
3 2 1 2 3
3 2 2 2 3
3 3 3 3 3
Solution:
```
num=int(input("Enter the number of rows:"))
n_list=[[0 for x in range(num)] for y in range(num)]
low=0
high=num-1
count=int((num+1)/2)
for i in range(count):
for j in range(low,high+1):
n_list[i][j]=count
for j in range(low+1,high+1):
n_list[j][high]=count
for j in range(high-1,low-1,-1):
n_list[high][j]=count
for j in range(high-1,low,-1):
n_list[j][low]=count
low = low+1
high = high-1
count=count-1
for i in range(num):
for j in range(num):
print(format(n_list[i][j],"1d"),end=" ")
```

print()

```
Enter the number of rows:5
3 3 3 3 3
3 2 2 2 3
3 2 1 2 3
3 2 2 2 3
3 3 3 3 3
```

Output of Q13

Q14. Write a python program to print the following pattern

```
1 1 1 1 1
1 2 2 2 1
1 2 3 2 1
1 2 2 2 1
1 1 1 1 1
```

Solution:

```python
num=int(input("Enter the number of rows:"))
n_list=[[0 for x in range(num)] for y in range(num)]
n=1
low=0
high=num-1
count=int((num+1)/2)
for i in range(count):
for j in range(low,high+1):
n_list[i][j]=n
for j in range(low+1,high+1):
n_list[j][high]=n
for j in range(high-1,low-1,-1):
n_list[high][j]=n
for j in range(high-1,low,-1):
n_list[j][low]=n
low = low+1
high = high-1
n=n+1
for i in range(num):
```

```
for j in range(num):
print(format(n_list[i][j],"1d"),end=" ")
print()
```

```
Enter the number of rows:5
1 1 1 1 1
1 2 2 2 1
1 2 3 2 1
1 2 2 2 1
1 1 1 1 1
```

Output of Q14

Q15.Write a python program to print triangle of numbers

1

1 2

1 2 3

1 2 3 4

1 2 3 4 5

Solution:

```
n=int(input("Enter the number of rows: "))
for i in range(1,n+1):
for j in range(1,i+1):
print(j, end=" ")
print()
```

Note: Replace "j" with "i" , "i**2" and "j**2" to observe interesting patterns

```
Enter the number of rows: 5
1
1 2
1 2 3
1 2 3 4
1 2 3 4 5
```

a) with "j"

b) with "i"

```
Enter the number of rows: 5
1
2 2
3 3 3
4 4 4 4
5 5 5 5 5
```

with "i"

Note: Try with"i**2" and "j**2" to observe interesting patterns

Q16. Write a python program to print the following pattern

```
1
2 1
3 2 1
4 3 2 1
5 4 3 2 1
```

Solution:

```
n=int(input("Enter the number of rows: "))
for i in range(1,n+1):
for j in range(i,0,-1):
print(j,end=" ")
print()
```

```
Enter the number of rows: 5
1
2 1
3 2 1
4 3 2 1
5 4 3 2 1
```

Output of Q16

Q17. Write the python program to draw the following pattern

```
1
2 3
4 5 6
7 8 9 10
11 12 13 14 15
```

Solution:

```
s=1
n=int(input("Enter the number of rows: "))
for i in range(1,n+1):
for j in range(1,i+1):
print(s,end=" ")
s += 1
print()
```

```
Enter the number of rows: 5
1
2 3
4 5 6
7 8 9 10
11 12 13 14 15
```

Output of Q17

Q18. Write a python program to draw the following pattern

```
1
3 2
6 5 4
10 9 8 7
15 14 13 12 11
```

Solution:

```
s=1
t=2
c=t
n=int(input("Enter the number of rows: "))
for i in range(2, n+2):
for j in range(s,t):
c -= 1
```

```
print(c,end=" ")
print()
s=t
t += i
c=t
```

```
Enter the number of rows: 5
1
3 2
6 5 4
10 9 8 7
15 14 13 12 11
```

Output of Q18

Q19. Write a python program to draw the following pattern

```
1 2 3 4 5
1 2 3 4
1 2 3
1 2
1
```

Solution:

```
n=int(input("Enter the number of rows: "))
for i in range(n,0,-1):
for j in range(1,i+1):
print(j,end="")
print()
```

```
Enter the number of rows: 5
12345
1234
123
12
1
```

Output of Q19

Q20. Write a python program to draw the following pattern
54321
5432
543
54
5
Solution:
num=int(input("Enter the number of rows:"))
for i in range(1,num+1):
for j in range(num,i-1,-1):
print(j,end="")
print()

```
Enter the number of rows:5
54321
5432
543
54
5
```

Output of Q20

Q21. Write a python program to draw the following pattern
5
45
345
2345
12345
Solution:
num=int(input("Enter the number of rows:"))
temp=num
for i in range(num,0,-1):
for j in range(i,num+1):
print(j,end="")
print()

```
Enter the number of rows :5
5
45
345
2345
12345
```

Output of Q21

Q22. Write a python program to draw the following pattern
1
2 6
3 7 10
4 8 11 13
5 9 12 14 15
Solution:
n=int(input("Enter the number of rows: "))
for i in range(n):
v = i+1
inc = n-1
for j in range(i+1):
print(v,end=" ")
v = v+inc
inc = inc-1
print()

```
Enter the number of rows: 5
1
2 6
3 7 10
4 8 11 13
5 9 12 14 15
```

Output of Q22

Q23. Write a python program to draw the following pattern
1
2 9
3 8 10
4 7 11 14
5 6 12 13 15
Solution:
n=int(input("Enter the number of rows: "))
for i in range(n):
for j in range(i+1):
v=0
for k in range(j):
v=v+n-k
if j%2==0:
print(v+i-j+1,end=" ")
else:
print(v+n-i,end=" ")
print()

```
Enter the number of rows: 5
1
2 9
3 8 10
4 7 11 14
5 6 12 13 15
```

Output of Q23

Q24. Write a python program to draw the following pattern
1
2 1
4 2 1
8 4 2 1
16 8 4 2 1
Solution:
n=int(input("Enter the number of rows: "))
for i in range(n):

```
for j in range(i,-1,-1):
print(2**j, end=" ")
print()
```

```
Enter the number of rows: 5
1
2 1
4 2 1
8 4 2 1
16 8 4 2 1
```

Output of Q24

Q25. Write a python program to draw the following pattern
1
1 2 1
1 2 4 2 1
1 2 4 8 4 2 1
Solution:
```
n=int(input("Enter the number of rows: "))
for i in range(1,n):
for j in range(0,i,1):
print(2**j,end=" ")
for k in range(j-1,-1,-1):
print(2**k,end=" ")
print()
```

```
Enter the number of rows: 5
1
1 2 1
1 2 4 2 1
1 2 4 8 4 2 1
```

Output of Q25

Q26. Write a python program to draw the following pattern

15
14 10
13 9 6
12 8 5 3
11 7 4 2 1
Solution:
def num(n1):
if n1==1:
return 1
return n1+num(n1-1)
n=int(input("Enter the number of rows:"))
k=num(n)
for i in range(n):
v=k-i
dec=n-1
for j in range(i+1):
print(v,end=" ")
v=v-dec
dec=dec-1
print()

```
Enter the number of rows:5
15
14 10
13 9 6
12 8 5 3
11 7 4 2 1
```

Output of Q26

Q27. Write a python program to print the following pattern
13579
3579
579
79
9
Solution:

```
Enter the number of rows:5
13579
3579
579
79
9
```

Output of Q27

Q28. Write a python program to print the given pattern

1
12
123
1234
12345
1234
123
12
1

Solution:

```
n=int(input("Enter the number:"))
for i in range(1,n+1):
for j in range(1,i+1):
print(j,end="")
print()
for i in range(n-1,0,-1):
for j in range(1,i+1):
print(j,end="")
print()
```

```
Enter the number:5
1
12
123
1234
12345
1234
123
12
1
```

Output of Q28

Q29. Write a python program to print the mirror image of pattern in Q24

Solution:

```python
n=int(input("Enter the number:"))
for i in range(1,n+1):
for j in range(n,i,-1):
print(" ",end="")
for j in range(1,i+1):
print(j,end="")
print()
for i in range(n-1,0,-1):
for j in range(i,n):
print(" ",end="")
for j in range(1,i+1):
print(j,end="")
print()
```

```
Enter the number:5
    1
   12
  123
 1234
12345
 1234
  123
   12
    1
```

Output of Q29

Q30. Write a python program to print the following pattern
1
121
12321
1234321
123454321
1234321
12321
121
1
Solution:
```
n=int(input("Enter the number:"))
for i in range(1,n+1):
for j in range(1,i+1):
print(j,end="")
for j in range(i-1,0,-1):
print(j,end="")
print()
for i in range(n-1,0,-1):
for j in range(1,i+1):
print(j,end="")
for j in range(i-1,0,-1):
print(j,end="")
```

print()

```
Enter the number:5
1
121
12321
1234321
123454321
1234321
12321
121
1
```

Output of Q30

Q31. Write a python program to print the following pattern
*
1
121
12321
1234321
123454321
1234321
12321
121
1
*

Solution:
```python
n=int(input("Enter the number:"))
print("*")
for i in range(1,n+1):
print("*",end="")
for j in range(1,i+1):
print(j,end="")
for j in range(i-1,0,-1):
```

```python
print(j,end="")
print("*",end="")
print()
for i in range(n-1,0,-1):
print("*",end="")
for j in range(1,i+1):
print(j,end="")
for j in range(i-1,0,-1):
print(j,end="")
print("*",end="")
print()
print("*")
```

```
Enter the number:5
*
*1*
*121*
*12321*
*1234321*
*123454321*
*1234321*
*12321*
*121*
*1*
*
```

Output of Q31

## CHAPTER THREE

ALPHABETICAL PATTERNS

Q1. Write a python program to print the following pattern

```
A
BB
CCC
DDDD
EEEEE
```

Solution:

```python
n=int(input("Enter the number of rows:"))
N=65
for i in range(0,n):
for j in range(0,i+1):
ch=chr(N)
print(ch,end="")
N += 1
print()
```

```
Enter the number of rows:5
A
BB
CCC
DDDD
EEEEE
```

Output of Q1

Q2. Write a python program to print the given pattern
A
BC
DEF
GHIJ
KLMNO
Solution:
n=int(input("Enter the number of rows:"))
N=65
for i in range(0,n):
for j in range(0,i+1):
ch=chr(N)
print(ch,end="")
N += 1
print()

```
Enter  the  number  of  rows:5
A
BC
DEF
GHIJ
KLMNO
```

Output of Q2

Q3. Write a python program to print the following pattern
A
AB
ABC
ABCD
ABCDE
Solution:
n=int(input("Enter the number of rows:"))
for i in range(0,n):
N=65
for j in range(0,i+1):

```
ch=chr(N)
print(ch,end="")
N=N+1
print()
```

```
Enter the number of rows:5
A
AB
ABC
ABCD
ABCDE
```

Output of Q3

Q4. Write a python program to draw the following pattern
ABCDE
ABCD
ABC
AB
A
Solution:
```
n=int(input("Enter the number of rows:"))
for i in range(n,0,-1):
N=65
for j in range(1,i+1):
ch=chr(N)
print(ch,end="")
N=N+1
print()
```

```
Enter the number of rows:5
ABCDE
ABCD
ABC
AB
A
```

Output of Q4

Q5. Write a python program to print the following pattern

A
BA
CBA
DCBA
EDCBA
Solution:

```
n=int(input("Enter the number of rows"))
for i in range(1,n+1):
for j in range(i,0,-1):
ch=chr(j+64)
print(ch,end="")
print()
```

```
Enter  the  number  of  rows5
A
BA
CBA
DCBA
EDCBA
```

Output of Q5

Q6. Write a python program to print the following pattern

A B C D E
F G H I J
K L M N O
P Q R S T
U V W X Y

```
size = 5
count = 0
for i in range(size):
for j in range(size):
print(chr(65 + count), end=" ")
```

```
# changing charater
count += 1
print()
```

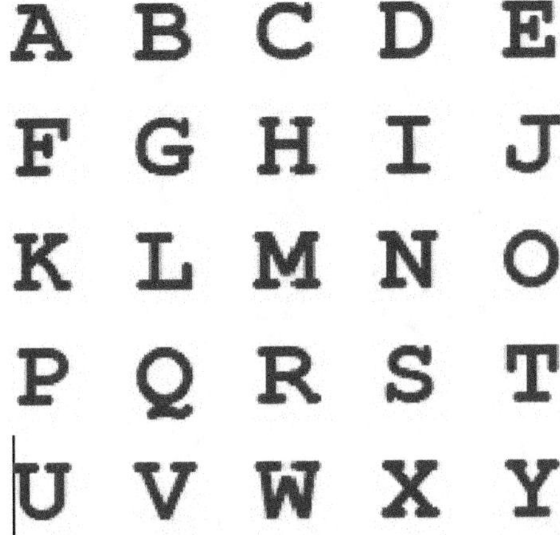

Output of Q6

Q7. Write a python program to print the following pattern

```
A A A A A
B B B B B
C C C C C
D D D D D
E E E E E
```

Solution:

```
size = 5
for i in range(size):
    for j in range(size):
        print(chr(65 + i), end=" ")
    print()
```

Solution:

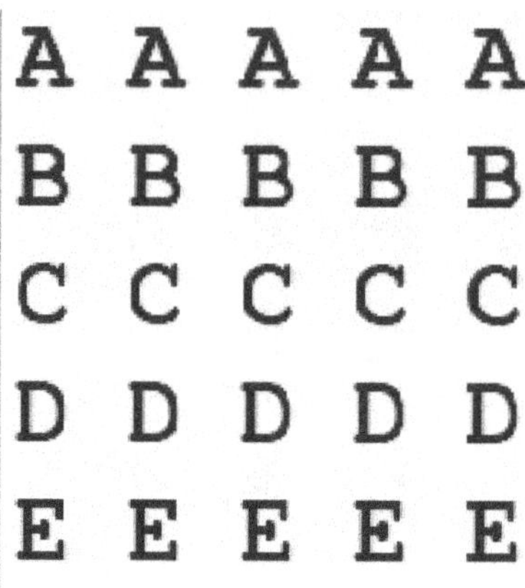

Output of Q7

Q8. Write a python program to print the following pattern

```
  A B C D E
A B C D E
A B C D E
A B C D E
A B C D E
```

Solution:

```
size = 5
for i in range(size):
for j in range(65, 65+size):
print(chr(j), end=' ')
print()
```

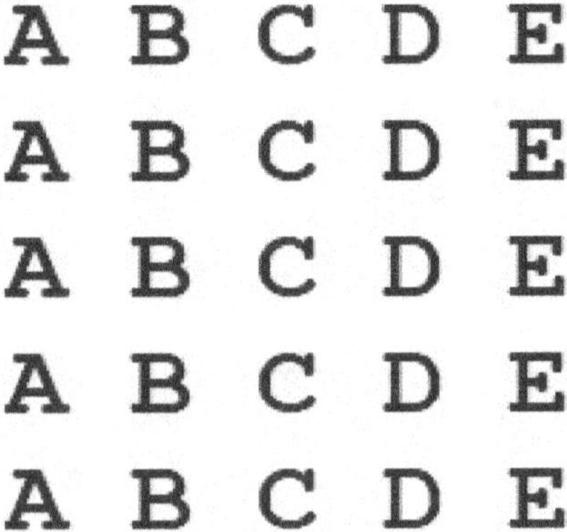

Output of Q8

Q9. Write a python program to print the following pattern
Solution:

```
n = 6
for i in range(1, n+1):
count = 0
for j in range(i):
# print alphabets only at start and end of the row
if j == 0 or j == i-1:
print(chr(65 + count), end=")
count += 1
# print only alphabets if it's last row
else:
if i != n:
print(' ', end=")
else:
print(chr(65 + count), end=")
count += 1
print()
```

```
A
AB
A  B
A    B
A      B
ABCDEF
```

Output of Q9

Q10. Write a python program to print the following pattern

```
    A
ABC
ABCDE
ABCDEFG
ABCDEFGHI
```

Solution:

```python
n = 5
for i in range(n):
    for j in range(n - i - 1):
        print(' ', end='')
    for k in range(2 * i + 1):
        print(chr(65 + k), end='')
    print()
```

<pre>
    A
   ABC
  ABCDE
 ABCDEFG
ABCDEFGHI
</pre>

Output of Q10

Q11. Write a python program to print the following pattern
Solution:

```python
n = 5
for i in range(n):
# printing spaces
for j in range(n - i - 1):
print(' ', end='')
    # printing alphabets
count = 0
for k in range(2 * i + 1):
# print alphabets at start and end of the row
if k == 0 or k == 2 * i:
print(chr(65 + count), end='')
count += 1
else:
if i == n - 1:
print(chr(65 + count), end='')
count += 1
else:
print(' ', end='')
print()
```

```
      A
    A   B
   A       B
  A           B
ABCDEFGHI
```

Output of Q11

Q12. Write a python program to print the following pattern
ABCDEFGHI
ABCDEFG
ABCDE
ABC
A

Solution:

```python
n = 5
for i in range(n):
# printing spaces
for j in range(i):
print(' ', end='')
# printing alphabet
for j in range(2*(n-i)-1):
print(chr(65 + j), end='')
print()
```

ABCDEFGHI
ABCDEFG
ABCDE
ABC
A

Output of Q12

Q13. Write a python program to print the following pattern

```
    A
ABC
ABCDE
ABCDEFG
ABCDEFGHI
ABCDEFG
ABCDE
ABC
A
```

Solution:

```python
n = 5
# upward pyramid
for i in range(n):
    for j in range(n - i - 1):
        print(' ', end='')
    for j in range(2 * i + 1):
        print(chr(65 + j), end='')
    print()
# downward pyramid
for i in range(n - 1):
    for j in range(i + 1):
        print(' ', end='')
```

```
for j in range(2*(n - i - 1) - 1):
print(chr(65 + j), end='')
print()
```

A
ABC
ABCDE
ABCDEFG
ABCDEFGHI
ABCDEFG
ABCDE
ABC
A

Output of Q13

Q14. Write a python program to print the following pattern
ABCDEFGHI
ABCDEFG
ABCDE
ABC
A
ABC
ABCDE
ABCDEFG
ABCDEFGHI

Solution:

```
n = 5
# downward pyramid
for i in range(n-1):
for j in range(i):
print(' ', end='')
for k in range(2*(n-i)-1):
print(chr(65 + k), end='')
print()
# uppward pyramid
for i in range(n):
for j in range(n-i-1):
print(' ', end='')
for k in range(2*i+1):
print(chr(65 + k), end='')
print()
```

```
ABCDEFGHI
 ABCDEFG
  ABCDE
   ABC
    A
   ABC
  ABCDE
 ABCDEFG
ABCDEFGHI
```

Output of Q14

Q15. Write a python program to print the right pascal pattern
Solution:

```python
n = 5
# upper triangle
for i in range(n):
for j in range(i + 1):
print(chr(65 + j), end="")
print()
# lower triangle
for i in range(n):
for j in range(n - i - 1):
print(chr(65 + j), end="")
print()
```

```
A
AB
ABC
ABCD
ABCDE
ABCD
ABC
AB
A
```

Output of Q15

Q16. Write a python program to print the heart shaped pattern
Solution:

```python
n = 6
# upper part of heart
for i in range(n//2, n, 2):
# print first spaces
for j in range(1, n-i, 2):
print(" ", end="")
# print first alphabet
for j in range(i):
print(chr(65 + j), end="")
# print second spaces
for j in range(1, n-i+1, 1):
print(" ", end="")
# print second alphabet
for j in range(i):
print(chr(65 + j), end="")
print()
    # lower part
for i in range(n, 0, -1):
for j in range(i, n):
print(" ", end="")
for j in range(i*2):
print(chr(65 + j), end="")
print()
```

```
ABC      ABC
ABCDE  ABCDE
ABCDEFGHIJKL
ABCDEFGHIJ
ABCDEFGH
ABCDEF
ABCD
AB
```

Output of Q16

## CHAPTER FOUR

ALPHABETS FROM A TO Z

Q1. Write a Python Program to print Capital Letter "A"
Solution:

```
for row in range(7):
for col in range(5):
if ((col==0 or col==4) and row!=0) or ((row==0 or row==3) and (col>0
and col<4)):
print("*", end="")
else:
print(end=" ")
print()
```

Output of Q1

Q2. Write a Python Program to print Capital Letter "B"
Solution:
for row in range(7):
for col in range(6):
if (col==0 or col==4) or ((row==0 or row==3 or row==6) and (col>0 and col<4)):
print("*", end="")
else:
print(end=' ')
print()

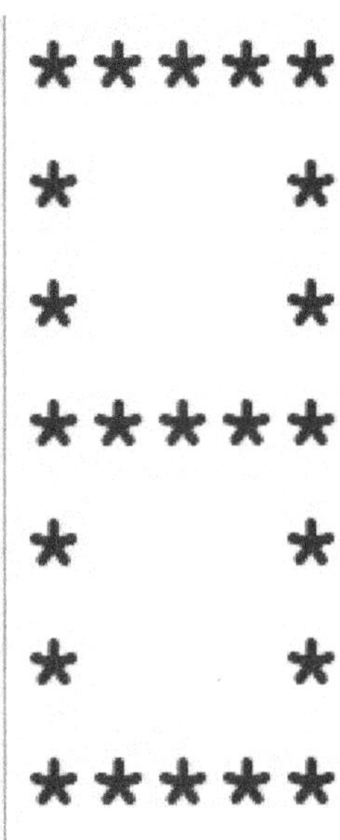

Output of Q2

Q3. Write a Python Program to print Capital Letter "C"
Solution:
```
for row in range(7):
for col in range(6):
if (col==0) or ((row==0 or row==6) and (col>0)):
print("*", end="")
else:
print(end=' ')
print()
```

Output of Q3

Q4. Write a Python Program to print Capital Letter "D"
Solution:
for row in range(7):
for col in range(5):
if (col==0) or ((col==4 and row!=0 and row!=6)) or ((row==0 or row==6)
and (col>0 and col<4)):
print("*", end="")
else:
print(end=' ')
print()

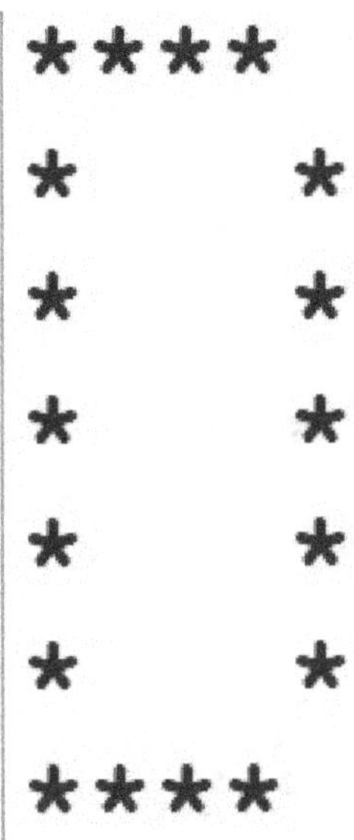

Output of Q4

Q5. Write a Python Program to print Capital Letter "E"
Solution:

```
for row in range(7):
for col in range(5):
if col==0 or ((row==0 or row==3 or row==6) and (col>0)):
print("*", end="")
else:
print(end=' ')
print()
```

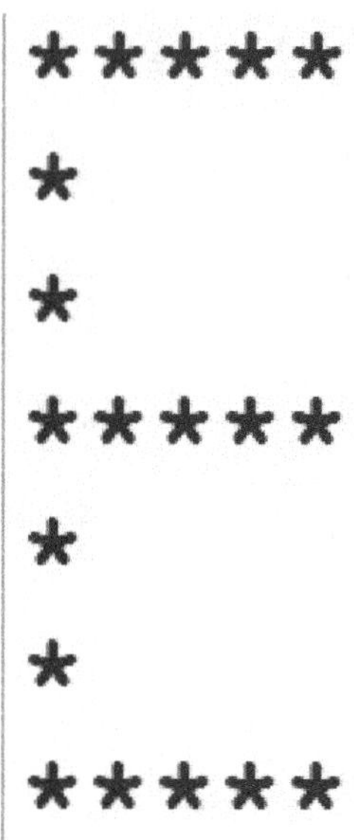

Output of Q5

Q6. Write a Python Program to print Capital Letter "F"
Solution:

```
for row in range(7):
for col in range(5):
if col==0 or ((row==0 or row==3) and (col>0)):
print("*", end="")
else:
print(end=' ')
print()
```

Output of Q6

Q7. Write a Python Program to print Capital Letter "G"
Solution:
    for row in range(7):
for col in range(6):
if col==0 or (col==4 and (row!=1 and row!=2)) or ((row==0 or row==6)
and (col>0 and col<4)) or (row==3 and (col==3 or col==5)):
print("*", end="")
else:
print(end=' ')
print()

Output of Q7

Q8. Write a Python Program to print Capital Letter "H"
Solution:
```
    for row in range(7):
for col in range(6):
if (col==0 or col==4) or (row==3 and (col>0 and col<4)):
print("*", end="")
else:
print(end=' ')
print()
```

Output of Q8

Q9. Write a Python Program to print Capital Letter "I"
Solution:
for row in range(7):
for col in range(5):
if col==2 or ((row==0 or row==6) and col!=2):
print("*", end="")
else:
print(end=' ')
print()

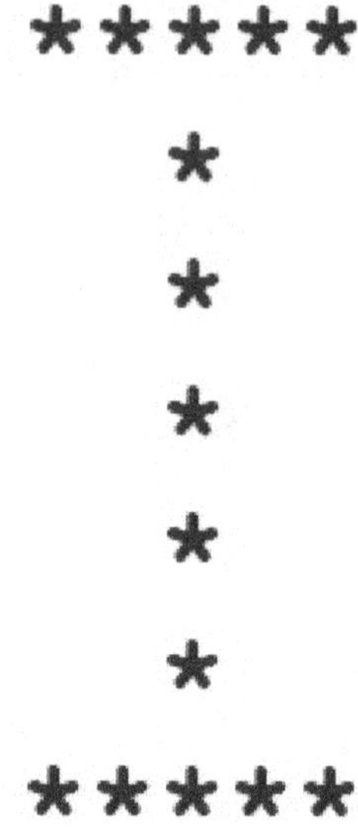

Output of Q9

Q10. Write a Python Program to print Capital Letter "J"
Solution:
for row in range(7):
for col in range(5):
if col==2 or (row==0 and col!=2) or (row==6 and col<2):
print("*", end="")
else:
print(end=' ')
print()

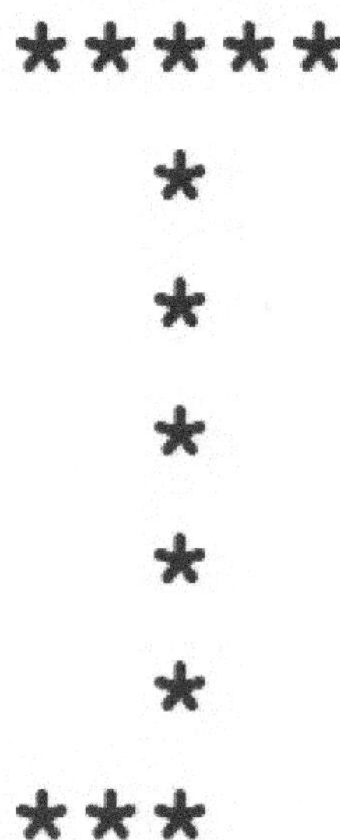

Output of Q10

Q11. Write a Python Program to print Capital Letter "K"
Solution:

```
i=0
j=4
for row in range(7):
for col in range(5):
if col==0 or (row==col+2 and col>1):
print("*", end="")
elif (row==i and col==j):
print("*", end="")
i=i+1
j=j-1
else:
print(end=' ')
print()
```

Output of Q11

Q12. Write a Python Program to print Capital Letter "L"
Solution:
for row in range(7):
for col in range(5):
if col==0 or (row==6 and col>0):
print("*", end="")
else:
print(end=' ')
print()

Output of Q12

Q13. Write a Python Program to print Capital Letter "M"
Solution:

```
for row in range(7):
for col in range(7):
if (col == 1 or col == 5 or (row == 2 and (col == 2 or col == 4)) or (row == 3 and col == 3)):
print("*", end="")
else:
print(end=' ')
print()
```

Output of Q13

Q14. Write a Python Program to print Capital Letter "N"
Solution:
```
    for row in range(6):
for col in range(6):
if (col == 0 or col == 5 or (row==col and (col>0 and col<5))):
print("*", end="")
else:
print(end=' ')
print()
```

Output of Q14

Q15. Write a Python Program to print Capital Letter "O"
Solution:

```
for row in range(7):
for col in range(5):
if ((col==0 or col==4) and (row!=0 and row!=6)) or ((row==0 or row==6)
and (col>0 and col<4)):
print("*", end="")
else:
print(end=' ')
print()
```

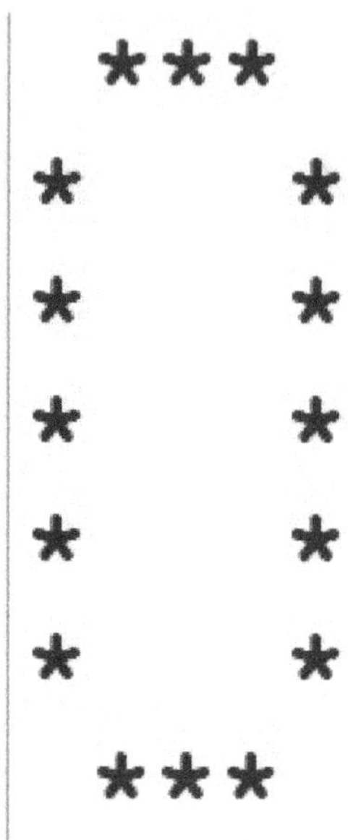

Output of Q15

Q16. Write a Python Program to print Capital Letter "P"
Solution:
for row in range(7):
for col in range(5):
if col==0 or (col==4 and (row==1 or row==2)) or (row==0 or row==3) and (col>0 and col<4):
print("*", end="")
else:
print(end=' ')
print()

Output of Q16

Q17. Write a Python Program to print Capital Letter "Q"
Solution:

```
for row in range(8):
for col in range(5):
if ((col==0 or col==4) and (row>0 and row<6)) or ((row==0 or row==6)
and (col>0 and col<4)) or (row==5 and col==1) or (row==7 and col==3):
print("*", end="")
else:
print(end=' ')
print()
```

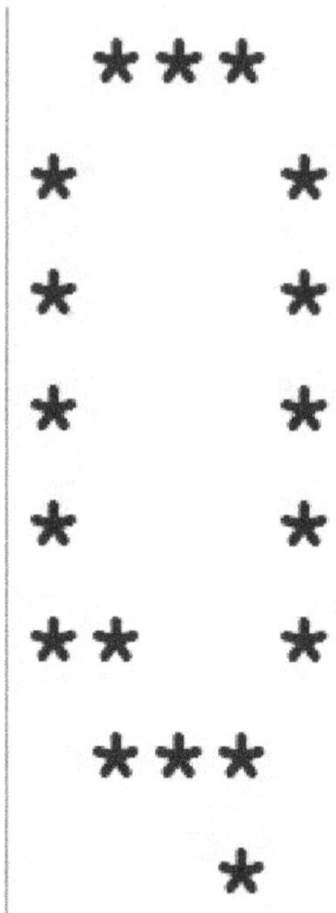

Output of Q17

Q18. Write a Python Program to print Capital Letter "R"
Solution:
for row in range(7):
for col in range(5):
if col==0 or (col==4 and (row!=0 and row!=3)) or ((row==0 or row==3)
and (col>0 and col<4)):
print("*", end="")
else:
print(end=' ')
print()

Output of Q18

Q19. Write a Python Program to print Capital Letter "S"
Solution:

```
for row in range(7):
for col in range(5):
if ((row==0 or row==3 or row==6) and (col>0 and col<4)) or (col==0 and (row>0 and row<3)) or (col==4 and (row>3 and row<6)):
print("*", end="")
else:
print(end=' ')
print()
```

Output of Q19

Q20. Write a Python Program to print Capital Letter "T"
Solution:

```
for row in range(7):
for col in range(5):
if col==2 or (row==0 and col!=2):
print("*", end="")
else:
print(end=' ')
print()
```

Output of Q20

Q21. Write a Python Program to print Capital Letter "U"
Solution:

```
for row in range(7):
for col in range(5):
if ((col==0 or col==4) and row!=6) or (row==6 and (col>0 and col<4)):
print("*", end="")
else:
print(end=' ')
print()
```

Output of Q21

Q22. Write a Python Program to print Capital Letter "V"
Solution:

```
    i=0
j=6
for row in range(4):
for col in range(7):
if row==col:
print("*", end="")
elif row==i and col==j:
print("*", end="")
i=i+1
j=j-1
else:
print(end=' ')
print()
```

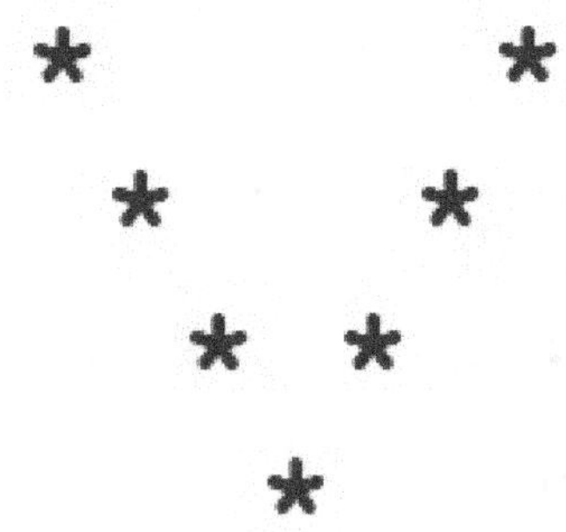

Output of Q22

Q23. Write a Python Program to print Capital Letter "W"
Solution:

```
    i=0
j=3
for row in range(4):
for col in range(7):
if col==0 or col==6 or (col==5 and row==2) or (col==4 and row==1):
print("*", end="")
elif row==i and col==j:
print("*", end="")
i=i+1
j=j-1
else:
print(end=' ')
print()
```

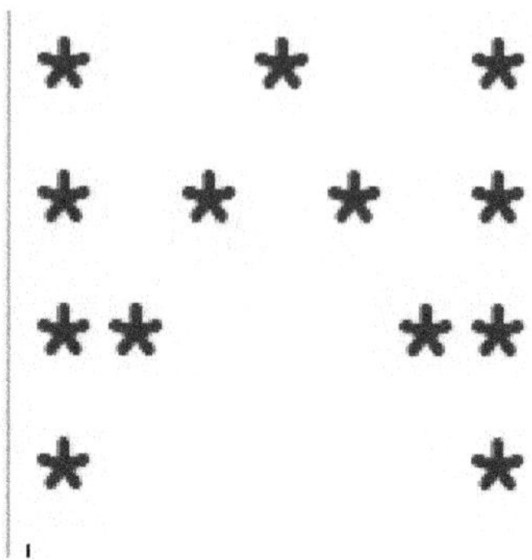

Output of Q23

Q24. Write a Python Program to print Capital Letter "X"
Solution:
i=0
j=4
for row in range(5):
for col in range(5):
if row==i and col==j:
print("*", end="")
i=i+1
j=j-1
elif row==col:
print("*", end="")
else:
print(end=' ')
print()

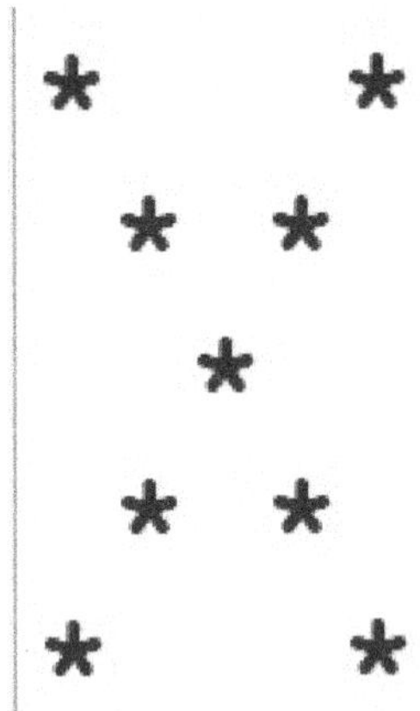

Output of Q24

Q25. Write a Python Program to print Capital Letter "Y"
Solution:

```
row in range(5):
for col in range(5):
if (col==2 and row>1) or (row==col and col<2) or (row==0 and col==4) or
(row==1 and col==3):
print("*", end="")
else:
print(end=' ')
print()
```

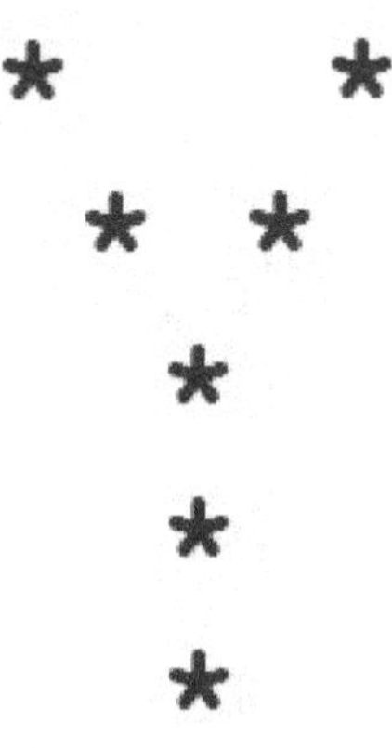

Output of Q25

Q26. Write a Python Program to print Capital Letter "Z"
Solution:

```
i=1
j=4
for row in range(0,6):
for col in range(0,6):
if row==0 or row==5:
print("*", end="")
elif row==i and col==j:
print("*", end="")
i=i+1
j=j-1
else:
print(end=' ')
print()
```

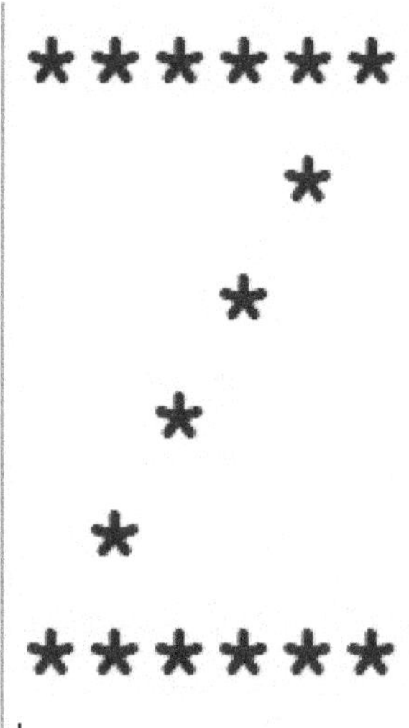

Output of Q26

## CHAPTER FIVE

MISCELLANEOUS

Q1. Write a Python Program to print Heart Shape
   Solution:

```
n = 6
for row in range(0,n):
for col in range(0,n+1):
if(row==0 and col%3!=0) or (row==1 and col%3==0) or (row-col==2) or
(row+col==8):
print('*',end='')
else:
print(' ',end='')

print()
```

Output of Q1

Q2. Write a Python Program to print Hut Shape
Solution:

```
def printHutStar(n):
for i in range(n):
for j in range(i + 1, n):
print(' ', end = '')
for j in range(0, 2 * i + 1):
print('*', end = '')
print()
for i in range(3):
for j in range(3):
print('*', end = '')
for j in range(2 * n - 7):
print(' ', end = '')
for j in range(3):
print('*', end = '')
print()
n = 7
printHutStar(n)
```

Output of Q2

Q3. Write a Python Program to print crown Shape
Solution:

```
n=3
for i in range(1, n+1):
for k in range(1, i+1):
print(" ",end="")
for j in range(1, i+1):
print("*",end="")
for k in range(1, 3*(n-i)+1):
print(" ",end="")
for j in range(1, 2*i):
print("*",end="")
for k in range(1, 3*(n-i)+1):
print(" ",end="")
for j in range(1, i+1):
print("*",end="")
print("\r")

for i in range(1, n//2+1):
for k in range(1, n+i):
print(" ",end="")
for j in range(1, 2*(n*2-i)+2):
print("*",end="")
print("\r")
```

Output of Q3

Q4. Write a Program to print left half diamond pattern using star(*) and hyphen(-) in Python

Solution:

```python
n = int(input("Enter the value n:"))
for i in range(0,n):
for j in range(1,n-i):
print(" ",end=")
if (i % 2)==0:
for k in range(0,i+1):
print("*",end=")
else:
for k in range(0,i+1):
print("-",end=")
print()
for i in range(n-1,0,-1):
for j in range(n,i,-1):
print(" ",end=")
if (i % 2)==0:
for k in range(i,0,-1):
print("-",end=")
else:
for k in range(i,0,-1):
print("*",end=")
print()
```

```
Enter the value n:5
         *
        --
       ***
      ----
     *****
      ----
       ***
        --
         *
```

Output of Q4

Q5. Write a Program to print right half diamond pattern using star(*) and hyphen(-) in Python

Solution:

```
n = int(input("enter the value of n:"))
for i in range(1,n+1):
if (i % 2)==0:
for k in range(1,i+1):
print("-",end='')
else:
for k in range(1,i+1):
print("*",end='')
print()
for i in range(n,1,-1):
if (i % 2)==0:
for k in range(i,1,-1):
print("*",end='')
else:
for k in range(i,1,-1):
print("-",end='')
print()
```

```
enter the value of n:5
*
--
***
----
*****
----
***
--
*
```

Output of Q5

Q6. Write a Program to print Triangle pattern using star(*) and hyphen(-) in Python
Solution:
```
n = int(input("enter the value of n:"))
for i in range(0,n):
for k in range(1,n-i):
print(" ",end='')
print("*",end='')
for j in range(0,i-1):
print("-",end='')
for j in range(0,i):
print("-",end='')
if i>0:
print("*",end='')
print()
```

```
enter the value of n:5
    *
   *-*
  *---*
 *-----*
*-------*
```

Output of Q6

Q7. Write a Program to print full diamond pattern using star(*) and hyphen(-) in Python

Solution:

```python
n = int(input("enter the value of n:"))
for i in range(1,n+1):
for k in range(0,n-i):
print(" ",end='')
if(i%2==1):
for j in range(0,2*i-1):
print("*",end='')
else:
for j in range(0,2*i-1):
print("-",end='')
print()
for i in range(n,1,-1):
for k in range(n,i-1,-1):
print(" ",end='')
if(i%2==1):
for j in range(2*i-2,1,-1):
print("-",end='')
else:
for j in range(2*i-2,1,-1):
print("*",end='')
print()
```

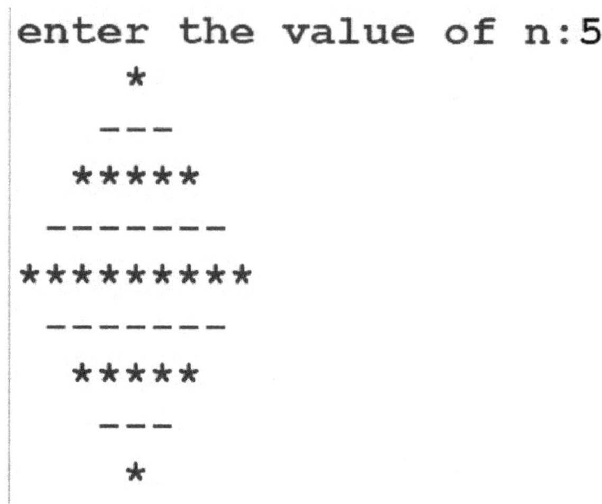

Output of Q7

Q8. Write a Python Program to print Swastika Pattern
Solution:
```python
n = 5
print("* ",end="")
for i in range(1, n-1):
print(" ",end="")
for i in range(1, n+1):
print("* ",end="")
print("\r")
for i in range(1, n-1):
print("* ",end="")
for j in range(1, n-1):
print(" ",end="")
print("*")
for i in range(1, n+n):
print("* ",end="")
print("\r")
for i in range(1, n-1):
for j in range(1, n):
print(" ",end="")
print("* ",end="")
```

```python
for j in range(1, n-1):
print(" ",end="")
print("* ")
    for i in range(1, n+1):
print("* ",end="")
for i in range(1, n-1):
print(" ",end="")
print("* ")
```

Output of Q8

Q9. Write a Python Program to print Star
Solution:
```python
    for i in range(9):
for j in range(13):
if i==2 or i==6 or i+j==6 or j-i==6 or i-j==2 or i+j==14:
print("*", end=')
```

```
else:
print(" ", end='')
print()
```

Output of Q9

Q10. Write a Program to print cristmas pattern in Python
Solution:
```
def triangleShape(n):
for i in range(n):
for j in range(n-i):
print(' ', end=' ')
for k in range(2*i+1):
print('*',end=' ')
print()
```

```
def poleShape(n):
for i in range(n):
for j in range(n-1):
print(' ', end=' ')
print('* * *')
    row = int(input('Enter number of rows: '))
    triangleShape(row)
triangleShape(row)
poleShape(row)
```

Enter number of rows: 4

```
                *
            *   *   *
          *   *   *   *   *
        *   *   *   *   *   *   *
                *
            *   *   *
          *   *   *   *   *
        *   *   *   *   *   *   *
            *   *   *
            *   *   *
            *   *   *
            *   *   *
```

Output of Q10

96